TOTALLY WEIRD ACTIVITY BOOKS

SUPER STRANGE

STORY STARTERS

Created by illustrator Mark Penta & writer T.M. Murphy

WEST
MARGIN
PRESS

HOW TO USE THIS BOOK

This book is full of super strange stories for you to read. Each of the stories ends with a cliffhanger.

Your job is to imagine what happens next! All you need is something to write with.

You can use the blank lines to finish your favorite story starters. If you need more space to write, there are more blank lines starting on page 52.

If you want, you can even draw additional characters or scenes!

Are you ready to read and write some totally weird stories?

Then turn the page and have fun!

ZAMIR GRAHAM AND THE MAGIC CLOSET

Zamir Graham's homework assignment was to research his heritage and create a family tree. It was also an excuse to stop by Grandma Graham's house for her awesome chocolate chip cookies.

One day it became more than a visit filled with sweet treats when she revealed a secret family story. One of Zamir's ancestors was actually a magician known as The Great Graham, who performed with the legendary Harry Houdini.

Zamir thought his grandmother was joking until she brought him to the cellar. There, he found himself standing before something called "The Great Graham's Magic Closet."

He rushed over, opened the curtain, and walked in.

In the background he heard Grandma Graham pleading, "No! No! Don't!"

It was too late. He couldn't believe his eyes. The first thing he saw was...

Continued on page _____

BOB MILKERSON IS THE LOBSTER WHISPERER

Bob Milkerson went fifty-seven years without ever eating lobster. That's why the Elvis impersonator from Nebraska was so excited when he booked a show in Maine.

Before his performance, Bob decided tonight would be the night. He was about to dig in when he noticed something.

The lobster was *moving*.

"Dude, you gotta get me outta here!"

Bob looked around. He couldn't believe it. Did the lobster just... speak?

I'm losing my mind! Bob thought.

"I'm not kidding, man. You have to help me! I gotta get outta here now!" the same voice said.

At that moment he got a wild idea, one that would make Bob Milkerson and his talking lobster famous throughout the world.

His idea was...

_____

_____

_____

_____

_____

_____

_____

_____

_____

Continued on page _____

FASHION GIRL'S MAGNIFICENT MALFUNCTIONING ADVENTURE

Created by several top designers and runway models, Rent-a-Robot's latest model, Fashion Girl, was the most popular and most expensive consultant on the market. Today she was hired to advise yet another rich teenager on prom night.

Since Fashion Girl was running late, her technician didn't check the robot's GPS before sending her out. A quick inspection would've revealed a malfunction indicating she was no longer programmed to appear at a billionaire's mansion in the Hamptons.

Instead, she was headed to one of the poorest sections of New York City, to the steps of a run-down apartment building that housed a very special teenage girl.

Fashion Girl knocked on the door and...

_____

_____

_____

_____

_____

_____

_____

_____

_____

_____

_____

_____

Continued on page ____

JOHNNY MARTINEZ AND HIS STRANGE VISION

Johnny Martinez was new to town, and like any new kid he was just trying to fit in.

But this became a great challenge during his first game for the Mansing Marvels. Something was happening to his vision. He saw multiples of EVERYTHING, resulting in him making three embarrassing errors.

The next day, Johnny went to the strange cabin office at the edge of town and was fitted with a pair of glasses from the eccentric Dr. Bateman.

Johnny got his vision back... but his new glasses also gave him the ability to see things that no one else could or even would want to see.

Johnny had no idea how to handle his new supernatural ability. He tried to go back and ask Dr. Bateman, but the doctor and his mysterious office had completely vanished into thin air.

Then on Johnny's first day of school, a girl wearing the same style of glasses approached him...

Continued on page _____

CUSTODIAN CARL AND THE RED ROOM

Carl had just been promoted to Head Custodian.

That meant he was now in charge of the key ring. He was excited, but not because of the promotion. No, Custodian Carl noticed that they forgot to take the crooked key bearing the initials *R.R.* off the ring.

The initials had a simple meaning behind them. They stood for "Red Room."

For nine years, Carl had wondered what was behind the door of the Red Room.

Finally he was about to find out...

Continued on page _____

MIA LEE IS THE FISHERGIRL

Mia Lee took ballet every afternoon. Her instructor thought she was a natural dancer, but Mia had other plans.

After every class, Mia would grab her pole and go fishing.

Her dream was to become a fisherman, or a "fisherwoman," as she liked to tell people. Her mother often described this as "a silly fantasy." Teased for her love of fishing, Mia felt sad and alone.

Maybe that was the reason she skipped her recital this time to stow away on the *Rosemarsh*, a fishing trawler headed to Alaska for King Crab season.

For two days as the boat was out at sea, Mia hid below deck. She was starving. She had to do something...

Continued on page _____

PACHUA KING
AND THE FEATHERED WATER SNAKES

Three days after Pachua King was born, two poisonous snakes slithered into his crib. Mrs. King didn't think her baby would survive the encounter, but she soon realized they were sent to protect him.

His Elders suggested naming him Pachua, meaning "feathered water snake." Since there was no water where he lived, it didn't really make sense. But the name stuck, and so did the snakes.

His Elders had big plans for Pachua, but when he turned eighteen, he said he wanted to see the world. He grabbed his skateboard, tied a string around his finger, and decided he wouldn't stop moving until the string came undone. It finally did.

Little did he know he was about to learn the significance of his name and the real reason the snakes were sent to his crib that fateful night...

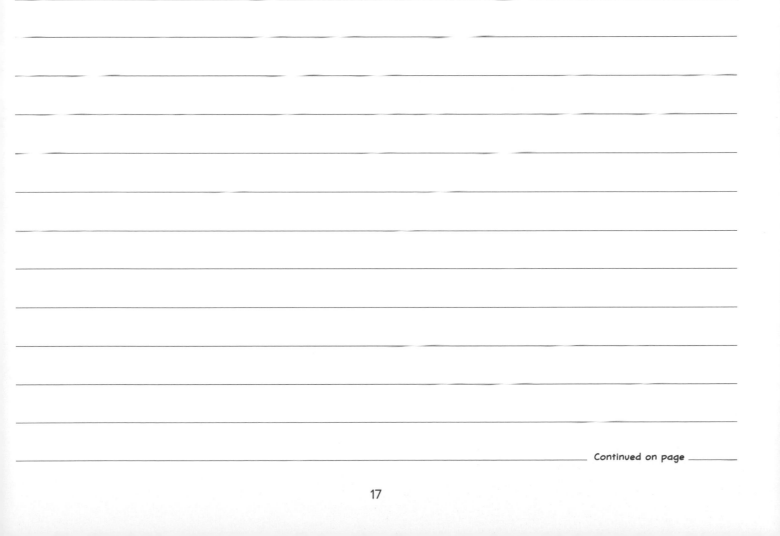

Continued on page ____

"GOOD GUY" GUS AND MR. GROUCHO

"Good Guy" Gus had done many odd jobs for the city's biggest crime family, but today's job was the oddest. He was to deliver a tied-up duck to a witness in an upcoming court trial with the strict message, "This is what will happen if you squawk."

The only problem was, Gus had never hurt a fly in his life, let alone a duck. He also never had a pet before. After meeting the duck, he instantly warmed up to the little fella and called him "Mr. Groucho."

Gus thought up a plan. He was going to...

_____

_____

_____

_____

_____

_____

_____

_____

_____

_____

_____

_____

_____

_____

_____

_____

_____

Continued on page _____

MARGUERITE LACROIX IS THE FORTUNE FINDER

Marguerite smiled all the time, but that didn't mean she was happy.

How could anyone who lied for a living be happy? Every time she had a customer, she would touch their hands, stare into the crystal ball, and tell them whatever they wanted to hear.

On the other hand, her mother, Lisette LaCroix, was the one who truly possessed "the gift." She had started the family business and forced the lifestyle onto Marguerite.

And so, Marguerite's smile was never real. That is, until the day she felt a pair of hands send a surge of energy through her body.

It was really happening, exactly how her mother had described it. The excitement and cosmic electricity flowed through her.

Marguerite peered into the ball and couldn't believe what she saw...

_____

_____

_____

_____

_____

_____

_____

_____

_____

_____

_____

_____

Continued on page _____

EDNA GLADSTONE BAKES A SPECIAL PIE

For most of her life, Edna had pleased everyone with her pies.

The County Fair didn't bother with blue ribbons anymore because Edna always won and never accepted them. It was no longer a challenge for her.

Edna was bored, and bored people sometimes do ridiculous things. She had no idea that adding a new "secret" ingredient to her famous blueberry pie would do anything more than give it a little zest. Her goal was just to give the judges something to talk about.

She was about to find out that this year's entry would do much more than that. She had no idea why there were news trucks parked in her driveway, but then she opened the front door.

And that's when it all began...

_____

_____

_____

_____

_____

_____

_____

_____

_____

_____

_____

_____

_____

Continued on page _____

GREGGOR MADDOX
IS THE GRAVE ROBBER

Greggor Maddox had no respect for the dead, stealing everything from them and then selling their jewelry and keepsakes to a shady pawn shop.

But when Greggor spotted the corpse's hand with a gold wedding band glistening in the moonlight, he knew that he had to have it for himself.

He put the ring on and it fit snuggly on his finger. Greggor felt a sudden burst of joy enter his heart, and he smiled. The rags he had been wearing became a tuxedo, and his worn boots were now polished black shoes.

The dark night sky became bright sunshine and the graveyard transformed into...

Continued on page _____

MAVIS MINDLEWARPE IS THE ALIEN DATER

Mavis Mindlewarpe was frustrated.

She felt there wasn't a good man to be found in her town, so she moved to the exotic Ponce de León Fountains Retirement Community with the hope of meeting someone out of this world.

Her wish came true the day the UFOs arrived. While the rest of the residents evacuated, she freshened her lipstick and picked an outfit that was sure to turn some cute alien heads. Mavis headed down to the beach with a gift for one of those very lucky visitors.

Little did she know the reaction from that gift would determine the future of mankind...

Continued on page _____

EDGAR CHEN AND THE GARDEN OF DREAMS

Edgar Chen owned Chen's Hardware. He had worked at the family business ever since he blew out his sixteen birthday candles.

If you were building a house, Edgar could tell you what nails to use and which aisle to find them. He had another dream in life, but he couldn't pursue it. His father would never allow him to do anything but continue the Chen's Hardware legacy.

But as Edgar locked up his store one evening, he realized he no longer could do that.

He wanted his own life, so he walked out the door and didn't look back.

Before he knew it, he had walked thirty miles. Finally, he reached a neighborhood that he'd never seen before. He approached a gate covered with flowers and spotted a woman beyond it working in her garden.

She smiled. "Edgar. You finally listened your heart." He couldn't believe his eyes. It was...

_____

_____

_____

_____

_____

_____

_____

_____

_____

Continued on page _____

LYDIA HOLMES IS THE TEENAGE SPY

Mr. Face instructed Lydia about her latest job. Of course, Mr. Face wasn't his real name. Ironically, that was one thing the two had in common.

Lydia Holmes was given her fake name the day *they* took her. All she knew about her past was what they told her—her parents had died in a car crash, and she possessed a rare gift for memorization.

Before the age of four, Lydia could recite all the U.S. Presidents and the fifty states. So then why can't she remember who she was and where she came from?

Deep down, she knew Mr. Face and her trainers were hiding something from her.

Was Lydia really working as a spy for her country, or had she been set up the whole time?

One day she decided it was time to find out the truth. She had a feeling that her new case might just help her do that.

Lydia opened the case file to see...

_____

_____

_____

_____

_____

_____

_____

_____

_____

Continued on page _____

EBENEZER HIGHTOWER AND THE SMILING DOLLS

Several decades ago, a fire gutted the Hightower Doll Factory. It was never rebuilt, making the ruins an eyesore for the people who lived in town.

Now, fifty years later, no one knew that deep inside a hidden cellar room in the abandoned factory, Ebenezer had returned to fix his mistake.

When he was ten years old, his bottle rocket had exploded and its fire had engulfed reams of fabric, destroying the factory. Ebenezer had fled town in shame. He became a drifter for a while, but now he drifted back to the factory. He would build new dolls for children and make things right with the town.

As Ebenezer inspected his latest doll, suddenly eyebrows appeared over her black button eyes. He hadn't sewn any eyebrows. He wiped his own eyes and squinted. The doll's fixed smile moved to form an open mouth.

"Ebenezer, you did it! You brought me to life, so I could finally give you this." The doll reached behind her back and...

Continued on page _____

LANCE SANDERS IS THE LEGENDARY LIFEGUARD

Lance Sanders was nicknamed "Mr. Box Office" for one simple reason—his movies made money. That's why he was the first choice for *Legendary Lifeguard*, a movie about a man who braves shark-infested waters and saves a swimmer only to find out he has rescued his childhood love.

During filming, Lance spotted the mechanical shark swimming toward his co-star on the horizon. That was the cue for his scene to begin, so he raced to the water and dove in.

When he got closer, he realized something truly terrifying—it was no mechanical shark, it was real, and it was heading straight for them...

Continued on page _____

TERRANCE SARGENT AND THE MAJESTIC BUTTERFLIES

Terrance Sargent couldn't call it "a midlife crisis" because he hadn't hit midlife yet. He was also happy and enjoyed his job selling high-end real estate in Manhattan.

But something compelled him that Sunday to put on his old favorite shirt, strap on his even older guitar, and play in the subway.

People smiled and clapped along, filling his money bowl before hopping the train and leaving him alone. At least, he thought he was alone. Suddenly, the dark hole of the tunnel brightened and thousands of butterflies appeared before him, dancing in the hot air to his song.

He instantly stopped playing, and that's when every butterfly landed on his old shirt. He felt their wings flutter all over his body. Before he knew it, they were lifting him off the ground.

"Where did you come from and where are you taking me?" he asked in awe...

Continued on page _____

SALLY JENKINS AND THE GHOST LETTER

Sally Jenkins had been a mail sorter at the post office for over thirty years. When she first started, she loved reading the faraway addresses, dreaming of what real-life stories were contained inside the letters.

But ever since e-mail came along, handwritten letters were becoming extinct. Other than the occasional letter to Santa Claus, nothing exciting ever came across her conveyor belt. That is, until the day she spotted *it*.

She was sixteen days, four hours, and six minutes from retirement when the yellow envelope caught her eye. It was postmarked July, 1978. There was no return address, but Sally recognized the handwriting. Her heart stopped for a second when she also realized the letter was addressed to her.

Sally had heard about letters that bounced around the system going years unopened. Postal workers called them "ghost letters"—and now she was holding one. She opened the letter and it read...

Continued on page _____

FERGUS BEDFORD THE SIXTH IS THE LIGHTHOUSE KEEPER

Fergus Bedford the Sixth was a name suited for royalty, and in the town of Arrowhead Point he was royalty to anyone who owned a boat.

Fergus was respected for being from a long line of Bedfords who manned the old lighthouse overlooking the mouth of the harbor. But he would be the last lighthouse keeper. Town officials decided that when he retired, they would install a high-tech automated system.

As he peered through his binoculars out at the Atlantic, Fergus felt that time had arrived. He knew he was getting old because his eyes were playing tricks on him. Could he really be seeing what he was seeing?

The scene was just like the legendary tale that had been passed from Fergus to Fergus. Now it was right before him, coming closer and closer...

Continued on page ___

HELEN RUSSELL
AND HER DEATHBED CONFESSION

Helen Russell had lived with a secret for over sixty years, and she didn't want to bring it to the grave.

But she had no family or friends left. All she had was the stranger standing at her bedside. She wondered if it would be worse to leave her secret with this nurse.

How would it affect the young woman's life? Helen pushed the thought from her mind and gave a faint smile.

"I've kept this story to myself for a very long time. I don't have anyone to tell it to, and I don't have much time to tell it. What you do with it will be your decision. So, pull up a chair and let me speak my final words..."

_____

_____

_____

_____

_____

_____

_____

_____

_____

_____

_____

_____

_____

Continued on page _____

SIMON SOUZA'S MYSTERIOUS JUNK

While everyone thought Simon Souza was a hoarder, Simon considered himself a collector, someone who preserved history. But the town officials ordered his totally weird store to be torn down and now a bulldozer was headed straight for his beloved treasures.

"Wait!" Simon yelled. "These objects are magical! If you destroy them—"

A crowd formed as Simon rushed to block the bulldozer. The driver turned off the engine. Simon continued, "Everyone listen to me! They will contact us with instructions!"

"Who will?" the driver blurted. Suddenly, the cordless rotary phone in front of Simon rang.

He picked up the receiver and held it out to the crowd, and an otherworldly voice boomed, "You must choose one of Simon's objects. Each one has a special power that will change your life."

As if in a trance, someone from the crowd stepped forward and picked...

Continued on page ____

THE CHANDER TWINS' MONSTER SECRET

Twins Reva and Varsha Chander were identical in every way except one: Reva had a prosthetic leg. She grew up doing everything her twin did, including playing on the varsity soccer team.

Reva lost her leg when she was ten. She never told her parents what occurred in the woods on that snowy night, or how she survived after getting lost for eight hours.

Varsha was the only other person who knew the story. Through twin telepathy, she not only felt the moment but also saw it in her head. She vowed to Reva to keep the secret.

They hoped the totally weird event was in the past, but as Reva took the penalty kick in the big game, a strange figure shot across the sky.

The Owl Woman, whose nest Reva had escaped from on that snowy night, had found her. Screaming players and fans scattered, but not the Chander Twins.

They knew exactly what to do...

Continued on page ____

READY FOR A CREATIVE CHALLENGE?

Make your own drawing here after you read the story starter to the right.

IRENE CAY AND THE MIRROR ON THE WALL

Irene Cay woke up from a deep sleep. She looked around the house and instantly felt dizzy with fear. This wasn't her home—the strange objects, the bright clothes, and the little girl playing with a doll.

Horror filled Irene's lungs with a scream, but the little girl didn't even react to the sound.

Fear overwhelmed Irene. She ran over and peered into a mirror for reassurance but saw nothing. Was she a ghost, or was the girl a ghost?

"I know you're here," the little girl said, breaking the silence. And what she said next was unbelievable...

_____

_____

_____

_____

_____

_____

_____

_____

_____

_____

_____

_____

_____

_____

_____

_____

Continued on page _____

READY FOR A CREATIVE CHALLENGE?

See the picture of the man of the left? Write your OWN story starter about him on the lines provided below. Who is he? What's his story?

Continued on page _____

How to Create Your Own Story Starters!

1 Get some supplies! (whichever you prefer!)

Something to write or draw with
Pencils, pens, eraser

a notebook and/or sketchbook
Lined or blank pages

or

a computer or tablet
a stylus pen

2 Observe the world around you! Story Starters are made by combining...

people

places

things

Hey! Don't forget us animals, insects and marine life!

psst! write about me!

When you see all this cool stuff, make notes and doodles so you'll remember them later!

3 — Develop your characters by asking yourself questions about them.

- How do they dress?
- What's their favorite hobby?
- Are they happy, sad, mad?

- What are their dreams?
- What do they say?
- What's their job?
- What's their backstory?

4 — ASK: "How can I make this character TOTALLY ORIGINAL?"

Here's the secret:

Look in your notes at your collection of people, places, and things. <u>Combine</u> the most unlikely choices to create a totally unique character and story!

EXAMPLE:

Chef — PERSON
ON the MOON — PLACE
plays a TUBA — THING
OWNS a NICE HORSE. — ANIMAL

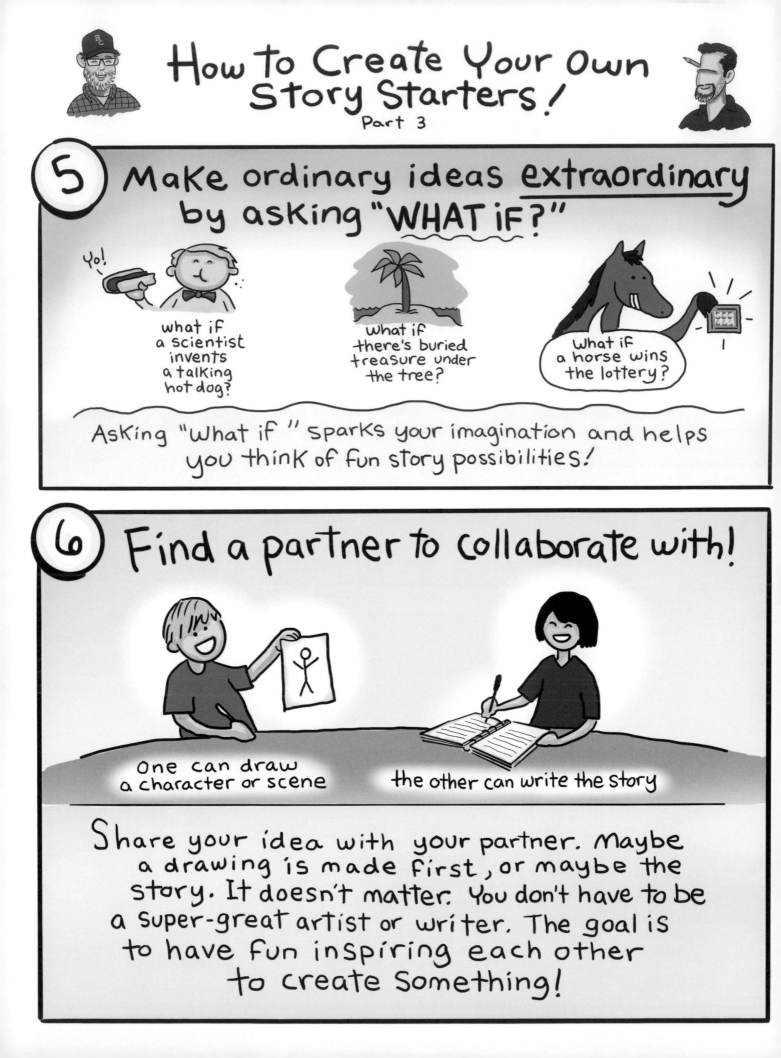

5 Make ordinary ideas extraordinary by asking "WHAT IF?"

Yo!

what if a scientist invents a talking hot dog?

what if there's buried treasure under the tree?

What if a horse wins the lottery?

Asking "What if" sparks your imagination and helps you think of fun story possibilities!

6 Find a partner to collaborate with!

One can draw a character or scene

the other can write the story

Share your idea with your partner. Maybe a drawing is made first, or maybe the story. It doesn't matter. You don't have to be a super-great artist or writer. The goal is to have fun inspiring each other to create something!

ACKNOWLEDGMENTS

Mark Penta: I'd like to thank my earliest childhood art teachers—Mrs. Rago, who always encouraged me, and Captain Bob Cottle, whose TV show inspired me to wake up at 6 a.m. and draw with him. A special thanks to my family for always supporting me.

T.M. Murphy: I would like to thank Bob Gallagher, Larry Palmacci, Peter McCarthy, Seton Murphy, and Sarah Murphy for their support in helping make this book come to life. I also want to thank Margaret Murphy for teaching me to follow my dreams. I'd like to dedicate this book to my wife, Jen, for being my greatest dream come true.

We want to thank our hardworking agent Murray Weiss of Catalyst Literary Management, and the creative crew at West Margin Press for believing in us.

ABOUT THE AUTHORS

T.M. Murphy is the author of the Belltown Mystery Series and *Saving Santa's Seals*. Murphy has been featured in *101 Highly Successful Novelists*, and chosen by *Cape Cod Life Magazine* as One of the 400 Cape Cod People Who Brighten Our Lives. He spends his winters touring schools and his summers teaching young writers at The Writers' Shack in his hometown of Falmouth, Massachusetts. Visit www.facebook.com/TheJustWriteItClass.

Mark Penta is a freelance illustrator and Hartford Art School graduate. His work has been published by Dell Magazines, Andrews McMeel, and featured on the Belltown Mystery book covers. He is the author/illustrator of several picture books, including *Cape Cod Invasion!* which was named a "Must-have product" by *Cape Cod Life Magazine*. He has taught drawing lessons to all ages, both privately and at schools like R.I.S.D. He also runs a fun and successful drawing service at private parties and corporate events. Visit www.MarkPenta.com.

Learn more about their Totally Weird Activity Books at
www.TotallyWeirdActivityBooks.com and
www.facebook.com/TotallyWeirdActivityBooks.

ISBN: 9781513134895

Printed in China
1 2 3 4 5 6 7 8 9 10

Published by West Margin Press®

WEST
MARGIN
PRESS

WestMarginPress.com

Proudly distributed by Ingram Publisher Services

WEST MARGIN PRESS
Publishing Director: Jennifer Newens
Marketing Manager: Alice Wertheimer
Project Specialist: Micaela Clark
Editor: Olivia Ngai
Design & Production: Rachel Lopez Metzger